Savvy

HOLD THE MEAT

VEGETARIAN
SANDWICHES

for
KIDS

written by
ALISON DEERING

illustrated by
BOB LENTZ

CAPSTONE PRESS
a capstone imprint

TO MY DAD, WHO TAUGHT ME THE BEAUTY OF A GREAT LUNCH SANDWICH, AND TO MY MOM, WHO STILL MAKES ME SANDWICHES NOW. — AD

TO THE SAUCEMAN, SORRY THERE ISN'T MORE RANCH DRESSING IN HERE. — BL

Savvy Books are published by
Capstone Press
1710 Roe Crest Drive, North Mankato, Minnesota 56003
www.mycapstone.com

Library of Congress Cataloging-in-Publication Data

Names: Deering, Alison, author.
Title: Hold the meat : vegetarian sandwiches for kids / by Alison Deering.
Description: North Mankato, Minnesota : Capstone Press, [2017] | Series:
   Savvy. Between the bread | Audience: Age 9–13. | Audience: Grade 4–6. |
   Includes bibliographical references and index.
Identifiers: LCCN 2017008311 | ISBN 9781515739197 (hardcover)
Subjects: LCSH: Vegetarian cooking. | Sandwiches. | LCGFT: Cookbooks.
Classification: LCC TX818 .D44 2017 | DDC 641.5/636—dc23
LC record available at https://lccn.loc.gov/2017008311

Designer: Bob Lentz
Creative Director: Heather Kindseth
Production Specialist: Tori Abraham

Printed in the United States of America.
010373F17

TABLE OF CONTENTS

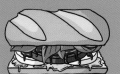

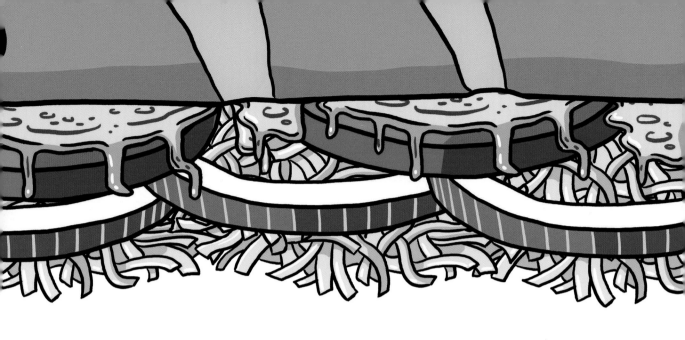

INTRODUCTION

(AKA WHAT IS A SANDWICH)

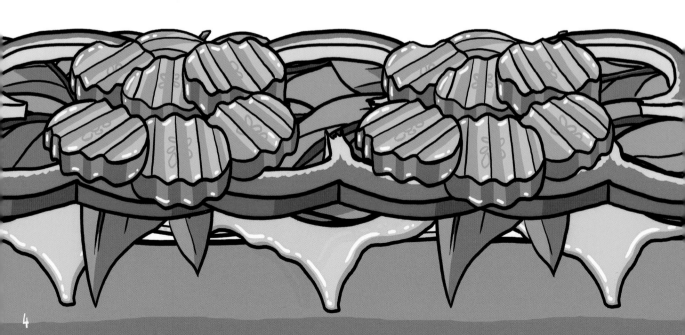

What is a sandwich? According to the United States Department of Agriculture, the "Product must contain at least 35 percent cooked meat and no more than 50 percent bread." But we have good news — for our purposes, a sandwich is whatever you make of it!

Your sandwich can be sweet or savory. It can be piled high or rolled up tightly. It can eaten for breakfast, lunch, dinner, or even dessert! But no matter what, a great sandwich starts with the basics — the ingredients. Bookend your kitchen creation with the bread of your choosing — wheat, white, rye . . . you name it! But don't forget that what's between the bread is just as important — veggies, cheese, and toppings can make or break a sandwich.

The beauty and genius of a delicious sandwich is that YOU as the chef and creator can make it anything you want it to be. And with this guidebook, you'll learn how to build the best vegetarian sandwiches ever.

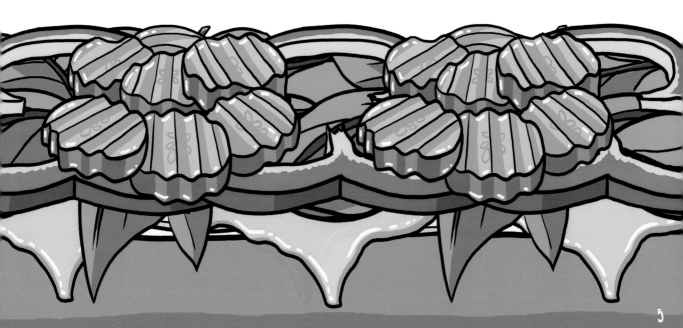

PB&J (& JELLY) (PEANUT BUTTER

Peanut butter and jelly sandwiches — more commonly known as PB&Js — are a sandwich staple around the country. Chances are good that you've eaten at least a few in your lifetime. And while a PB&J might sound basic, it's anything but. The sweet jelly combined with the sticky, savory peanut butter make this classic sandwich practically irresistible.

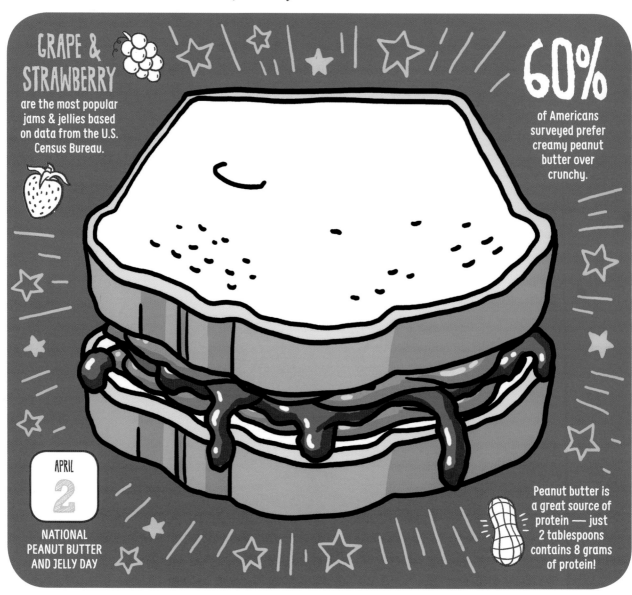

GRAPE & STRAWBERRY are the most popular jams & jellies based on data from the U.S. Census Bureau.

60% of Americans surveyed prefer creamy peanut butter over crunchy.

APRIL
2

NATIONAL PEANUT BUTTER AND JELLY DAY

Peanut butter is a great source of protein — just 2 tablespoons contains 8 grams of protein!

WHITE BREAD

WHOLE WHEAT BREAD

ENGLISH MUFFIN

TORTILLA

PEANUT BUTTER

PRO TIP!

Keeping your sandwich from getting soggy is all about the technique — spread both pieces of bread with peanut butter and then add the jelly to the middle.

GRAPE JELLY

STRAWBERRY JAM

APRICOT PRESERVES

ALMOND BUTTER, sunflower seed butter, and other substitutes can be used in place of peanut butter if you have a peanut allergy.

PEANUT BUTTER

CHUNKY PEANUT BUTTER

Try it with

WHITE BREAD

POTATO CHIPS

MILK

MORE PB IDEAS ON PGS. 8-9

PB&J (PEANUT BUTTER & JELLY)

THE HISTORY OF THE PB&J

PB&J sandwiches may be a lunchbox staple in schools across the country, but that wasn't always the case. In fact, peanut butter used to be considered a delicacy. In the early 1900s it was served at upscale parties and fancy tearooms in New York. (Think peanut-butter-and-pimento and peanut-butter-with-watercress sandwiches.)

It wasn't until 1920 that the price of peanut butter dropped, and it became available to the masses, in part because sugar was added to the mix. Then, in the late 1920s, Gustav Papendick invented a process for slicing and wrapping bread, which meant kids (just like you!) could finally make their own sandwiches. Suddenly peanut butter sandwiches became a household staple.

Here's a brief breakdown of the life of a PB&J:

1884 — Marcellus Gilmore Edson, a Canadian, invents and patents peanut paste, made by milling roasted peanuts between two heated surfaces.

1893 — Peanut butter starts to gain popularity at the Chicago World's Fair.

1895 — Dr. John Harvey Kellogg patents a process for creating peanut butter from raw peanuts. He markets it as a healthy protein substitute for patients without teeth.

1901 — The first official reference to a peanut butter & jelly sandwich in the U.S. appears in *The Boston Cooking-School Magazine of Culinary Science and Domestic Economics*, thanks to Julia Davis Chandler.

1903 — Dr. Ambrose Straub of St. Louis, Missouri, patents a peanut-butter-making machine.

1920s — Sliced bread is invented! This invention takes sandwiches to the next level. Now kids can make sandwiches on their own.

1920s–1930s — Commercial peanut butter brands, including Peter Pan and Skippy, are introduced.

1930s — Peanut butter sandwiches become popular during the Great Depression, when many people needed a hearty, filling meal on the cheap. Peanut butter, which is packed with protein, became a more affordable substitute for meat.

1940s — Both peanut butter and jelly were part of U.S. soldiers' military rations; it's said that soldiers added jelly to their peanut butter sandwiches to make it more palatable. When those soldiers returned home, they helped the PB&J grow in popularity.

WE DARE YOU!

Peanut butter is great on its own, but a sandwich savant like you is probably ready to take it to the next level. Think you can handle the weird, the gross, the amazing, and everything in between? Here are just a few out-there options to experiment with . . . if you dare!

MAYO

CHEESE PUFFS

RAISINS

BUTTER

KETCHUP

FRIED EGG

AMERICAN CHEESE

LETTUCE

PICKLES

POTATO CHIPS

9

CUCUMBER CREAM CHEESE

Cucumber cream cheese sandwiches are a staple of tea time, but the good news is, tea sandwiches aren't limited to just high tea. You can enjoy this light, tasty treat anytime you want! This version is made with thinly sliced crunchy cucumbers and smooth cream cheese. The best part is, you can have more than one! (Ask an adult for help or permission when you're using a sharp knife.)

2—3
The number of bites it should take to eat a tea sandwich.

Cucumber sandwiches originated in the United Kingdom.

FINGER FOOD
Tea sandwiches are meant to be a light snack before the main meal.

MORE TEA SANDWICHES!
• Prosciutto & asparagus
• Egg salad (see pg. 36)
• Tomato & cheddar

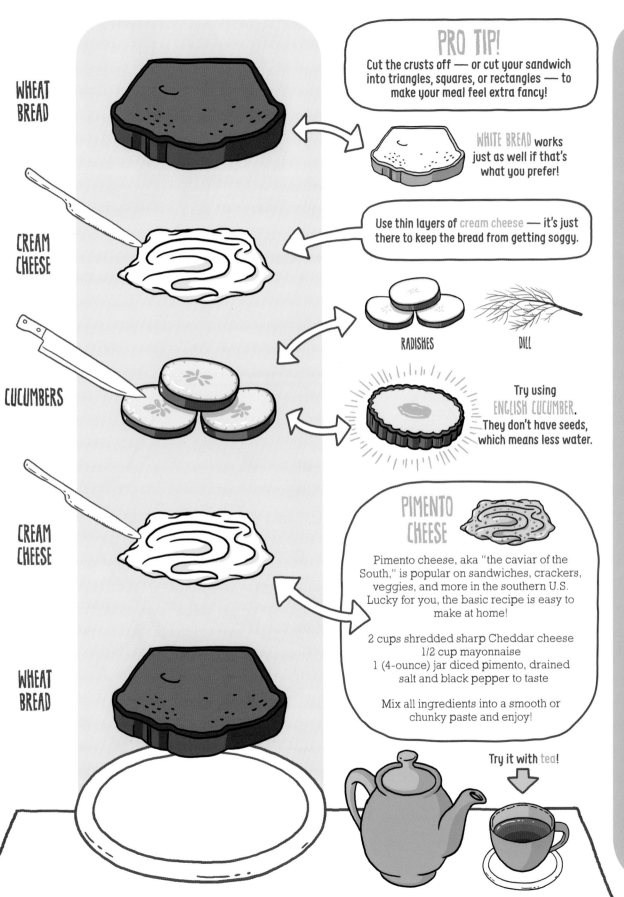

HUMMUS

Hummus isn't just a dip for fresh veggies — with the amount of protein chickpeas pack, hummus has the strength to stand as the base for its own sandwich! Pile on crunchy veggies, like cucumber and sprouts, to contrast hummus's creamy texture. If you're feeling fancy, you can add falafel to your sandwich as well.

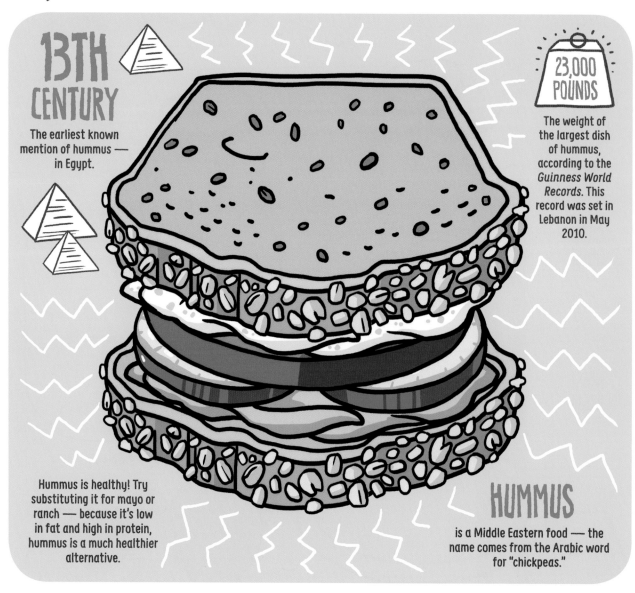

13TH CENTURY

The earliest known mention of hummus — in Egypt.

23,000 POUNDS

The weight of the largest dish of hummus, according to the *Guinness World Records*. This record was set in Lebanon in May 2010.

Hummus is healthy! Try substituting it for mayo or ranch — because it's low in fat and high in protein, hummus is a much healthier alternative.

HUMMUS

is a Middle Eastern food — the name comes from the Arabic word for "chickpeas."

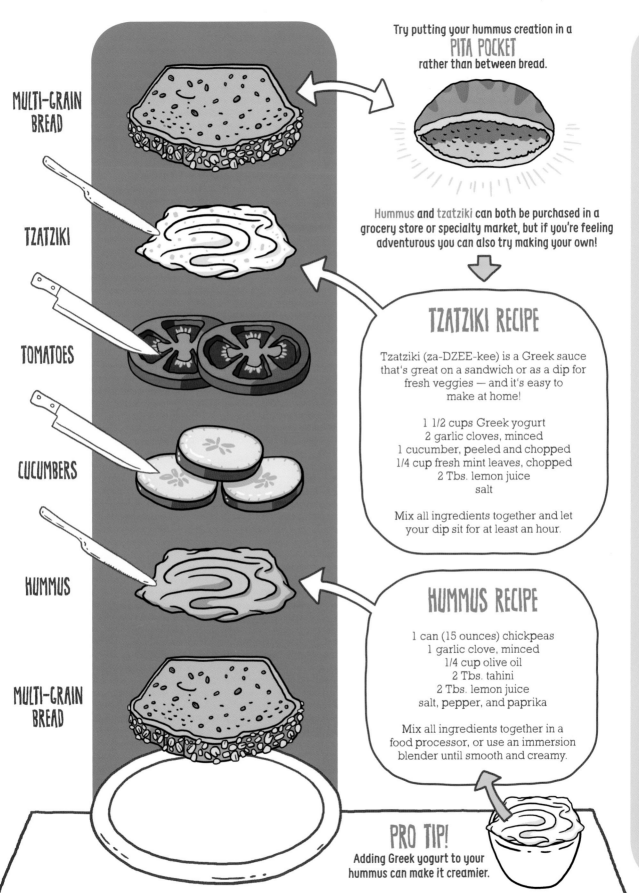

MULTI-GRAIN
BREAD

TZATZIKI

TOMATOES

CUCUMBERS

HUMMUS

MULTI-GRAIN
BREAD

Try putting your hummus creation in a
PITA POCKET
rather than between bread.

Hummus and tzatziki can both be purchased in a grocery store or specialty market, but if you're feeling adventurous you can also try making your own!

TZATZIKI RECIPE

Tzatziki (za-DZEE-kee) is a Greek sauce that's great on a sandwich or as a dip for fresh veggies — and it's easy to make at home!

1 1/2 cups Greek yogurt
2 garlic cloves, minced
1 cucumber, peeled and chopped
1/4 cup fresh mint leaves, chopped
2 Tbs. lemon juice
salt

Mix all ingredients together and let your dip sit for at least an hour.

HUMMUS RECIPE

1 can (15 ounces) chickpeas
1 garlic clove, minced
1/4 cup olive oil
2 Tbs. tahini
2 Tbs. lemon juice
salt, pepper, and paprika

Mix all ingredients together in a food processor, or use an immersion blender until smooth and creamy.

PRO TIP!
Adding Greek yogurt to your hummus can make it creamier.

HUMMUS

CAPRESE

Pizza, pasta, caprese — all the greats originate in Italy. The same goes for this delicious sandwich, a between-the-bread version of *insalata Caprese*, which literally translates to "salad of Capri" — a nod to the Italian isle on which it originated. A classic caprese sandwich is all about the ingredients: juicy tomatoes, fragrant basil, and fresh mozzarella. Typically served on a crusty baguette, this tasty treat is a vegetarian delight.

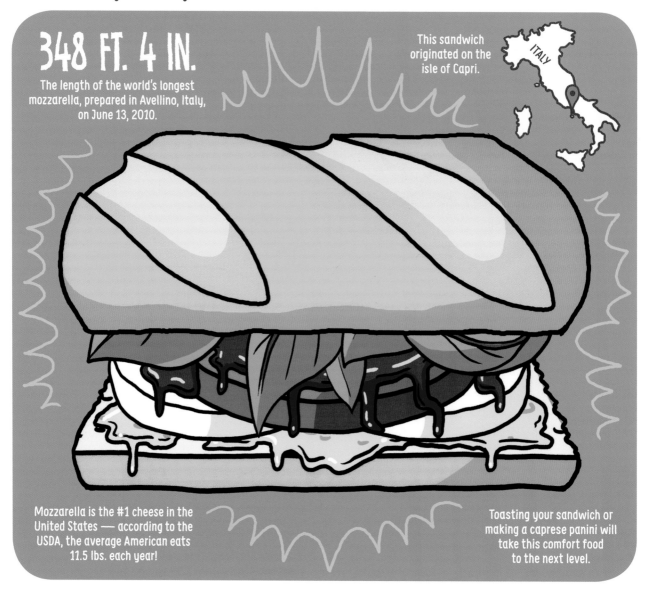

348 FT. 4 IN.

The length of the world's longest mozzarella, prepared in Avellino, Italy, on June 13, 2010.

This sandwich originated on the isle of Capri.

ITALY

Mozzarella is the #1 cheese in the United States — according to the USDA, the average American eats 11.5 lbs. each year!

Toasting your sandwich or making a caprese panini will take this comfort food to the next level.

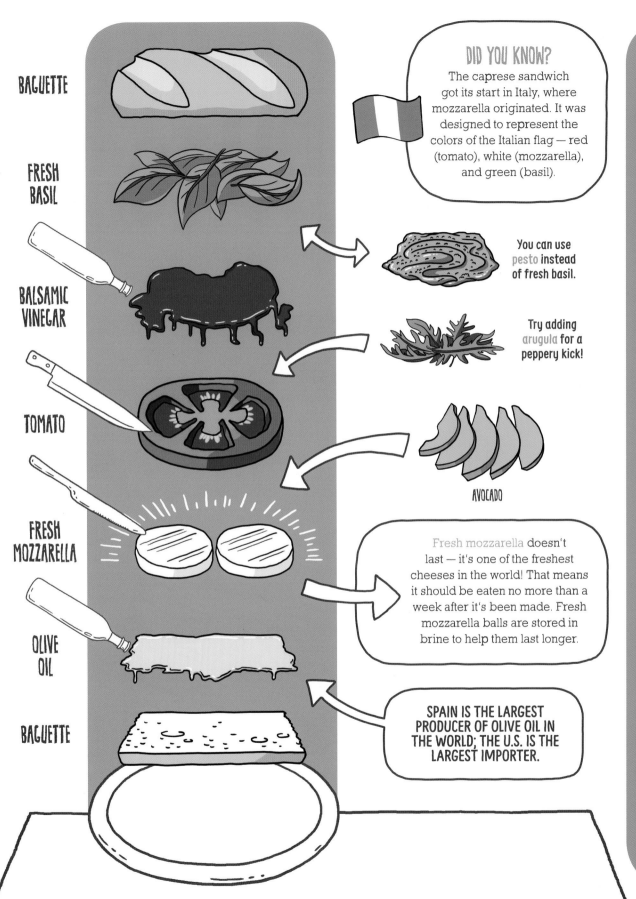

BAGUETTE

FRESH BASIL

BALSAMIC VINEGAR

TOMATO

FRESH MOZZARELLA

OLIVE OIL

BAGUETTE

DID YOU KNOW?
The caprese sandwich got its start in Italy, where mozzarella originated. It was designed to represent the colors of the Italian flag — red (tomato), white (mozzarella), and green (basil).

You can use pesto instead of fresh basil.

Try adding arugula for a peppery kick!

AVOCADO

Fresh mozzarella doesn't last — it's one of the freshest cheeses in the world! That means it should be eaten no more than a week after it's been made. Fresh mozzarella balls are stored in brine to help them last longer.

SPAIN IS THE LARGEST PRODUCER OF OLIVE OIL IN THE WORLD; THE U.S. IS THE LARGEST IMPORTER.

STUFFED FRENCH TOAST

French toast isn't strictly a breakfast food anymore. It's easy to take your leftover French toast and turn it into a delicious sandwich and brand-new meal. Similar to the Monte Cristo, minus the meat, this stuffed version combines sweet strawberries and cream cheese for a scrumptious stuffed sandwich.

4TH CENTURY

The first recipe for French toast appears in *Apicius*, a cookbook with a collection of ancient Roman recipes.

The French name "pain perdu" means "lost bread" — this refers to the fact that French toast is a way to use up stale bread, which would otherwise be lost.

NOVEMBER
28

NATIONAL FRENCH TOAST DAY

FRENCH TOAST

CREAM CHEESE

STRAWBERRIES

POWDERED SUGAR

FRENCH TOAST

STRAWBERRIES

CREAM CHEESE

FRENCH TOAST

DID YOU KNOW?
French toast is also known as German toast, eggy bread, gyspy toast, french-fried bread, and more!

Try substituting different fruits — these would also work well:

BANANAS

PEACHES

PEARS

APPLES

PRO TIP!
If you're making your French toast fresh, day-old bread is best.

Don't have fresh strawberries? Try using preserves or jam instead.

Sprinkle more powdered sugar on top, and serve with a side of syrup for dipping.

ROASTED VEGGIE

You don't have to fire up the grill or oven to enjoy a roasted veggie sandwich. Like many sandwiches, the beauty is in the simplicity — roasted vegetables from a jar or can will work just as well. And you pick what sounds good — roasted red peppers, zucchini, mushrooms, and more can be used to beef up this meatless meal. Spinach, arugula, or romaine lettuce adds some crunch, while tangy goat cheese rounds things out.

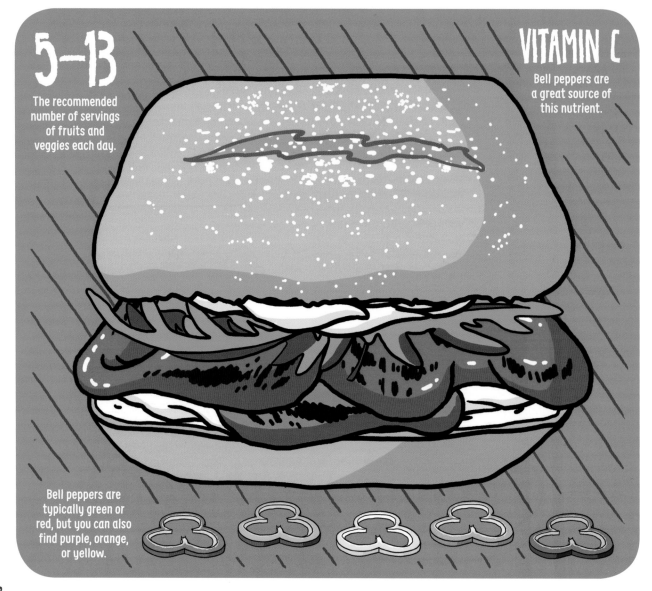

5–13
The recommended number of servings of fruits and veggies each day.

VITAMIN C
Bell peppers are a great source of this nutrient.

Bell peppers are typically green or red, but you can also find purple, orange, or yellow.

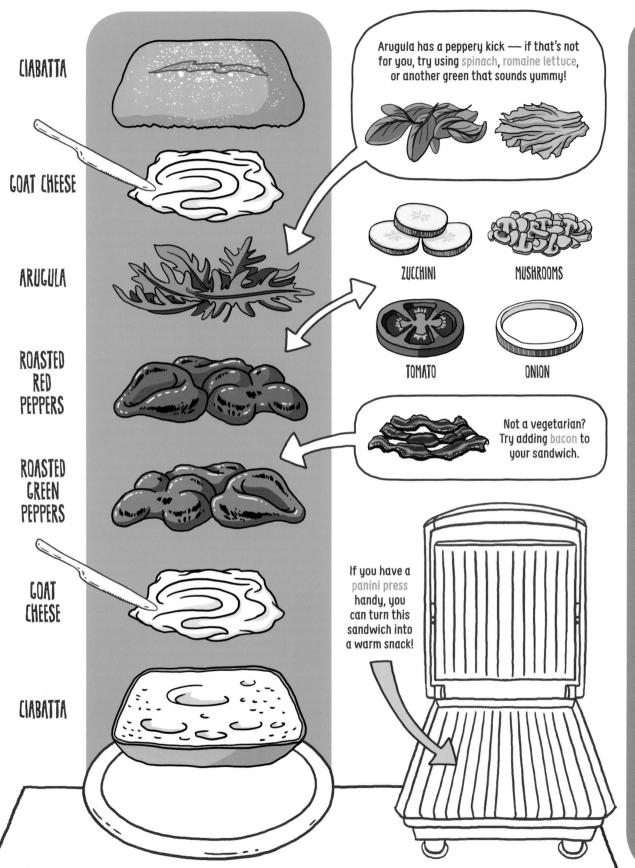

CIABATTA

GOAT CHEESE

ARUGULA

ROASTED
RED
PEPPERS

ROASTED
GREEN
PEPPERS

GOAT
CHEESE

CIABATTA

Arugula has a peppery kick — if that's not for you, try using spinach, romaine lettuce, or another green that sounds yummy!

ZUCCHINI

MUSHROOMS

TOMATO

ONION

Not a vegetarian? Try adding bacon to your sandwich.

If you have a panini press handy, you can turn this sandwich into a warm snack!

PB&B (PEANUT BUTTER & BANANA)

Served warm and sometimes called an "Elvis Sandwich" or simply the "Elvis," the PB&B uses toasted bread, peanut butter, and mashed or sliced bananas, depending on your personal preference. You can also add honey to take your sandwich to the sweeter side! No matter what your modifications, the PB&B is a great source of protein and potassium — perfect for days you have a big test at school or a big game after.

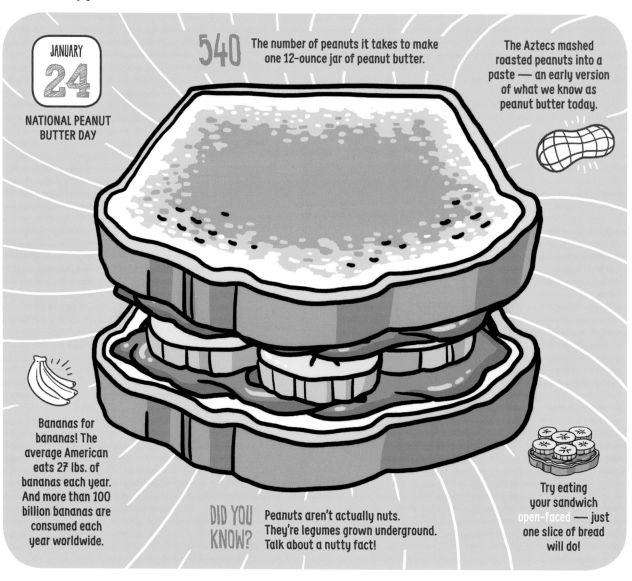

JANUARY
24

NATIONAL PEANUT BUTTER DAY

540 The number of peanuts it takes to make one 12-ounce jar of peanut butter.

The Aztecs mashed roasted peanuts into a paste — an early version of what we know as peanut butter today.

Bananas for bananas! The average American eats 27 lbs. of bananas each year. And more than 100 billion bananas are consumed each year worldwide.

DID YOU KNOW? Peanuts aren't actually nuts. They're legumes grown underground. Talk about a nutty fact!

Try eating your sandwich open-faced — just one slice of bread will do!

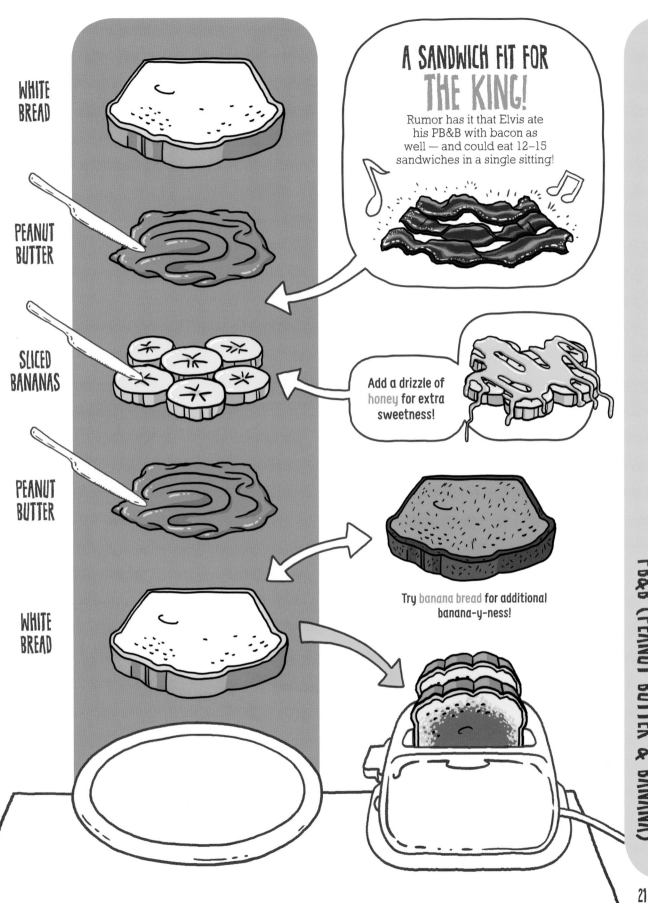

WHITE BREAD

PEANUT BUTTER

SLICED BANANAS

PEANUT BUTTER

WHITE BREAD

A SANDWICH FIT FOR THE KING!

Rumor has it that Elvis ate his PB&B with bacon as well — and could eat 12–15 sandwiches in a single sitting!

Add a drizzle of honey for extra sweetness!

Try banana bread for additional banana-y-ness!

PB&B (PEANUT BUTTER & BANANA)

GRILLED CHEESE

There's no better comfort food than bread and cheese — and grilled? Well that's just taking it to the next level. This classic sandwich can be made on the stove, in the oven, or using a panini press if you want to get extra fancy. Try experimenting with different types of cheese, and pair your sandwich with tomato soup for the ultimate comfort-food meal.

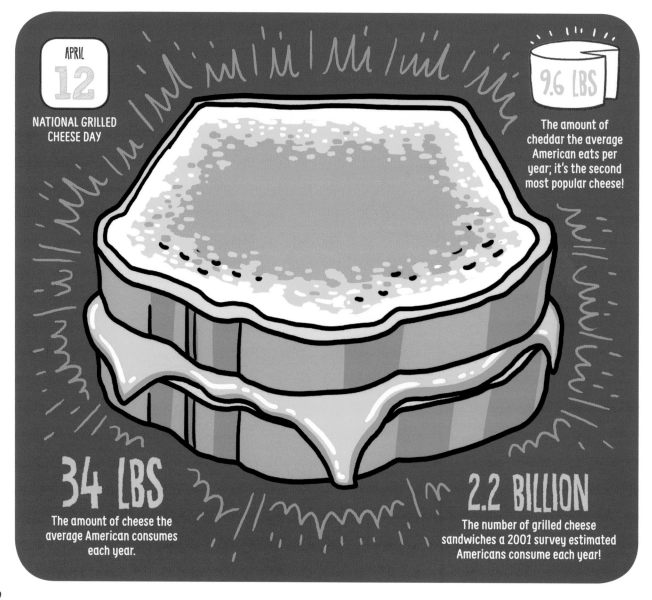

APRIL 12

NATIONAL GRILLED CHEESE DAY

9.6 LBS

The amount of cheddar the average American eats per year; it's the second most popular cheese!

34 LBS

The amount of cheese the average American consumes each year.

2.2 BILLION

The number of grilled cheese sandwiches a 2001 survey estimated Americans consume each year!

WHITE BREAD

Don't forget to butter the outside of both slices of bread before grilling — that's crucial to get the outside of your sandwich nice and crispy!

The Brits do it differently — the cheese-and-pickle sandwich is popular across the pond! It's not usually toasted, but we say, why not?

AMERICAN CHEESE

WHITE BREAD

Use Texas toast for an extra-thick grilled cheese.

Try multi-grain bread for extra crunch and nuttiness.

Use mayo in place of butter for grilling.

Grill your sandwich for a couple minutes on each side, until the bread is golden-brown and the cheese is melted.

Try it with

TOMATO SOUP

MILK

MORE GRILLED CHEESE **ON PGS. 24–25**

GRILLED CHEESE

THE HISTORY OF THE GRILLED CHEESE

Cooked bread and cheese has been popular since ancient times, but the modern grilled cheese, now a staple in homes across the country — and one of the best comfort foods around! — didn't get its start until much later.

Journey with us down the grilled-cheese timeline:

1920s — Inexpensive sliced bread and American cheese are made available to the masses. (Cheese sandwiches at this time are mostly served open faced, with one slice of bread and grated American cheese.)

1930s — During the Great Depression, the "cheese dream" (an open-faced grilled cheese sandwich) becomes increasingly popular as an easy, inexpensive way to feed friends and family during Sunday supper.

1940s — During WWII, Navy cooks make countless grilled cheese sandwiches, as instructed by official government-issued cookbooks.

1949 — Kraft singles are introduced.

1960s — "Grilled cheese" finally makes an appearance in print. Before this, these sandwiches were mostly known as "toasted cheese" or "melted cheese" sandwiches.

1965 — Supermarkets start stocking Kraft singles; this is around the same time the second slice of bread was added to the grilled cheese, making it a more filling meal.

WE DARE YOU!

A grilled cheese is great on its own, but a sandwich savant like you is probably ready to take it to the next level. Think you can handle the weird, the gross, the amazing, and everything in between? Here are just a few out-there options to experiment with . . . if you dare!

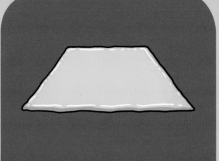

APPLE PIE FILLING

HOT SAUCE

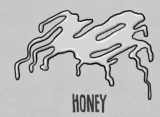
SPICY PICKLES

CRUNCHY PEANUT BUTTER

HONEY

APRICOT JELLY

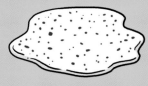
GRAVY

POTATO CHIPS

RANCH DRESSING

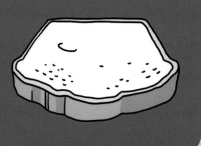
BANANAS

MAC AND CHEESE

Macaroni and cheese is great fresh — but what do you do with that day-old stuff? Reheated mac and cheese is never quite as good as the original . . . right? Think again! This mac and cheese sandwich is made with leftovers in mind! Grab some cold mac and cheese from the fridge, sandwich it between some bread, grill it up, and you're good to go! (Cold leftover mac works best since it will hold its shape better — perfect for a grilled sandwich!)

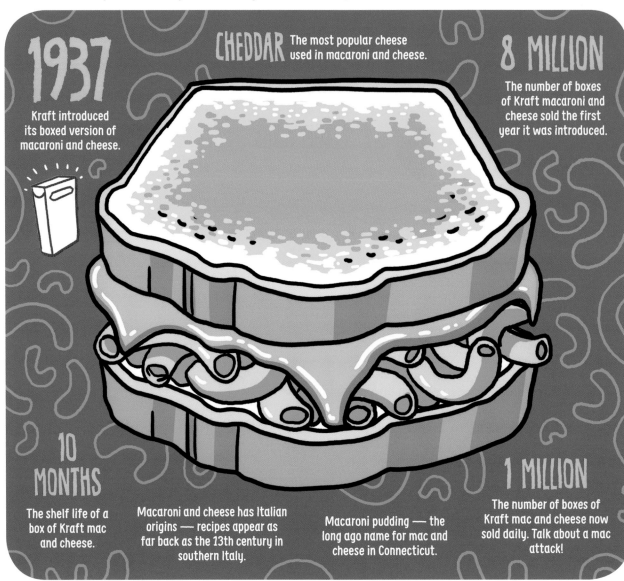

1937
Kraft introduced its boxed version of macaroni and cheese.

CHEDDAR The most popular cheese used in macaroni and cheese.

8 MILLION
The number of boxes of Kraft macaroni and cheese sold the first year it was introduced.

10 MONTHS
The shelf life of a box of Kraft mac and cheese.

Macaroni and cheese has Italian origins — recipes appear as far back as the 13th century in southern Italy.

Macaroni pudding — the long ago name for mac and cheese in Connecticut.

1 MILLION
The number of boxes of Kraft mac and cheese now sold daily. Talk about a mac attack!

WHITE BREAD

AMERICAN CHEESE

MAC AND CHEESE

WHITE BREAD

Don't forget to butter the outside of both slices of bread before grilling — that's crucial to get the outside of your sandwich nice and crispy!

Try using Texas toast or garlic bread in place of white bread for a heartier sandwich.

Make your mac and cheese sandwich your own by adding sliced tomato and/or cooked broccoli!

Grill your sandwich for a couple minutes on each side, until the bread is golden-brown and the cheese is melted.

RUMOR HAS IT . . .

Thomas Jefferson, one of America's founding fathers, might also be the man behind mac and cheese in the states. While visiting France and Italy, Jefferson fell in love with macaroni. He enjoyed the dish so much that he arranged to bring noodle recipes and a pasta machine back to America. (He later had both macaroni and parmesan cheese imported to use at his home, Monticello.) Jefferson even served mac and cheese at a state dinner in 1802, during his term as president.

(Jefferson was hardly the first to invent macaroni and cheese, though — the earliest known recipe was written down in 1769.)

ULTIMATE GRILLED CHEESE

Ready to take the cheese factor to the next level? The ULTIMATE grilled cheese piles on not one, not two, not three or four — but FIVE types of cheese. That's five layers of gooey, creamy goodness. Prepare your palate, because this is one sandwich not for the faint of heart.

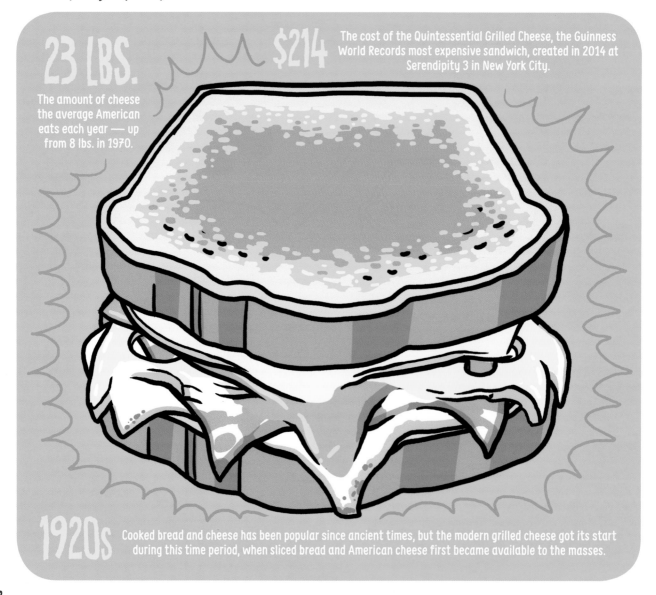

23 LBS.
The amount of cheese the average American eats each year — up from 8 lbs. in 1970.

$214
The cost of the Quintessential Grilled Cheese, the Guinness World Records most expensive sandwich, created in 2014 at Serendipity 3 in New York City.

1920s
Cooked bread and cheese has been popular since ancient times, but the modern grilled cheese got its start during this time period, when sliced bread and American cheese first became available to the masses.

SOURDOUGH BREAD

Don't forget to butter the bread before grilling! Add garlic salt to your sandwich for extra pizazz.

PROVOLONE CHEESE

CUSTOMIZE IT!

Try swapping out any of these cheeses for some of your other favorites:

CHEDDAR CHEESE

PEPPER JACK

SWISS CHEESE

BRIE

COLBY-JACK CHEESE

GOUDA

MUENSTER

MOZZARELLA CHEESE

HAVARTI

SOURDOUGH BREAD

AMERICAN

Grill your sandwich for a couple minutes on each side, until the bread is golden-brown and the toppings are gooey.

Try it with

TOMATO SOUP

MILK

ARTICHOKE = AND = CHEESE

Spinach-artichoke dip is often the hit of the party, and now it can be the star of your sandwich. The best part is, you don't need fresh artichokes to whip up this easy and delicious meal — use canned or frozen to simplify this sandwich. Then layer as much cheese as you can handle and heat up on the stove for a cheesy, delicious treat.

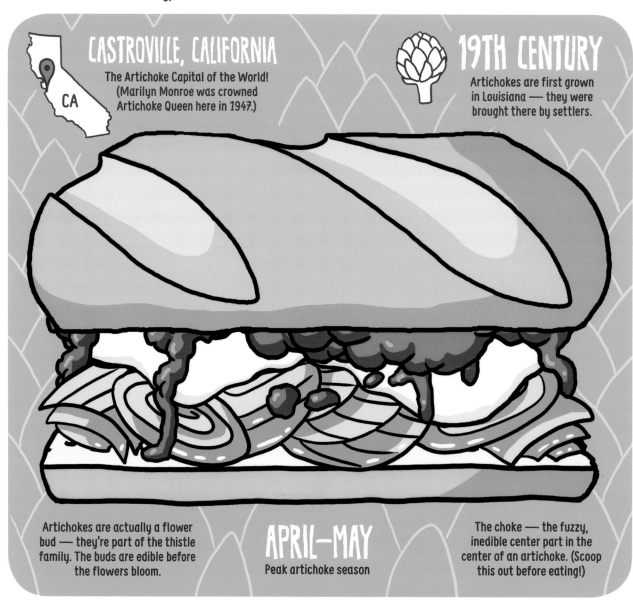

CASTROVILLE, CALIFORNIA

The Artichoke Capital of the World! (Marilyn Monroe was crowned Artichoke Queen here in 1947.)

19TH CENTURY

Artichokes are first grown in Louisiana — they were brought there by settlers.

Artichokes are actually a flower bud — they're part of the thistle family. The buds are edible before the flowers bloom.

APRIL–MAY

Peak artichoke season

The choke — the fuzzy, inedible center part in the center of an artichoke. (Scoop this out before eating!)

FRENCH BREAD

Pesto **also works well with** spinach artichoke **sandwiches!**

MARINARA SAUCE

Add parmesan **or** cream cheese **to make this sandwich even cheesier!**

PROVOLONE CHEESE

Add spinach **to create a handheld version of spinach-artichoke dip!**

PRO TIP!

Place your artichokes on a baking sheet and pop them in a 425° oven for 15–30 minutes to roast them. Then layer them on your sandwich to help melt the cheese!

ARTICHOKES

FRENCH BREAD

Or use a panini press!

EGG AND CHEESE

Breakfast is the most important meal of the day, but this egg and cheese sandwich isn't strictly an early morning treat — you can make and eat this cheesy delight morning, noon, or night! The best part? You can customize your sandwich however you'd like. Load up on veggies like tomatoes, onions, cucumbers, avocado and more to make your sanwich an even more filling meal!

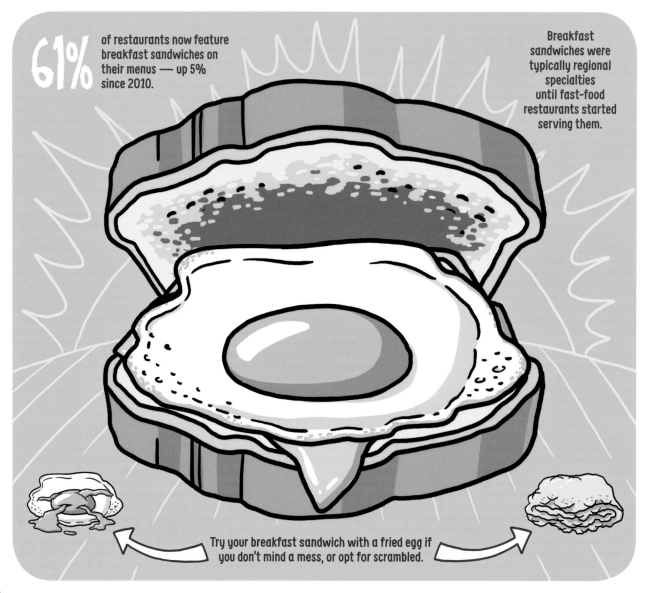

61% of restaurants now feature breakfast sandwiches on their menus — up 5% since 2010.

Breakfast sandwiches were typically regional specialties until fast-food restaurants started serving them.

Try your breakfast sandwich with a fried egg if you don't mind a mess, or opt for scrambled.

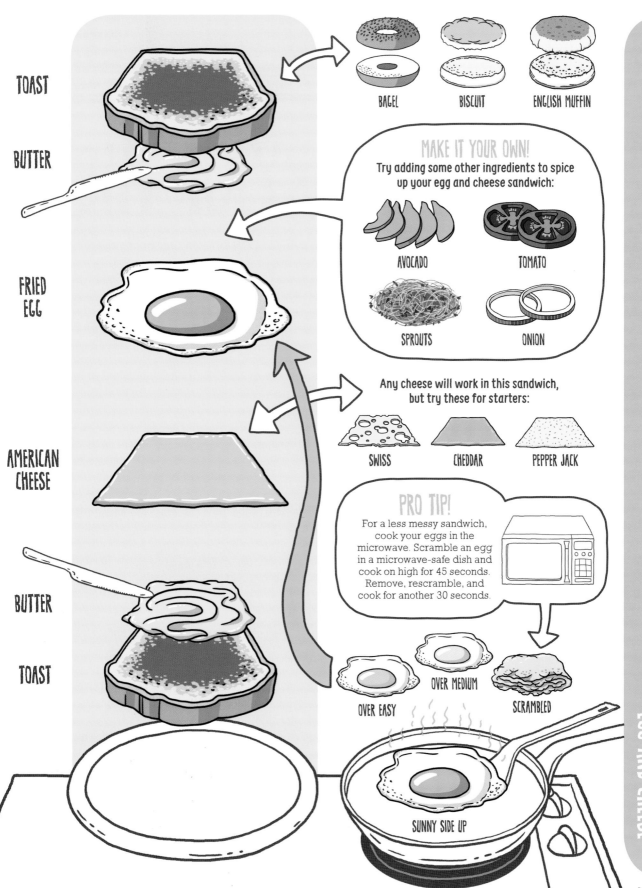

TOAST

BAGEL BISCUIT ENGLISH MUFFIN

BUTTER

MAKE IT YOUR OWN!
Try adding some other ingredients to spice up your egg and cheese sandwich:

AVOCADO TOMATO

SPROUTS ONION

FRIED EGG

Any cheese will work in this sandwich, but try these for starters:

SWISS CHEDDAR PEPPER JACK

AMERICAN CHEESE

PRO TIP!
For a less messy sandwich, cook your eggs in the microwave. Scramble an egg in a microwave-safe dish and cook on high for 45 seconds. Remove, rescramble, and cook for another 30 seconds.

BUTTER

OVER EASY OVER MEDIUM SCRAMBLED

TOAST

SUNNY SIDE UP

EGG AND CHEESE

33

THE HISTORY OF THE EGG SANDWICH

Journey with us down the egg sandwich timeline:

19TH CEN. — London factory workers grab breakfast sandwiches from street vendors on their way to work. These are originally called "bap" sandwiches after the rolls used to hold the fillings.

POST CIVIL WAR — American pioneers eat breakfast sandwiches on their long westward journeys, although the sandwiches aren't reserved as breakfast food. (And the added ingredients are likely a way to disguise less-than-fresh eggs.)

1897 — The first known "breakfast sandwich" recipe, using stale bread, chopped meat, milk, and egg, is published in an American cookbook, *Breakfast, Dinner and Supper, or What to Eat and How to Prepare It.*

1969 — Jack in the Box starts serving up an egg, meat, and cheese breakfast sandwich on an English muffin.

1971 — Herb Peterson, an advertising executive, invents the Egg McMuffin and starts selling it at his restaurant. He later introduces the sandwich to McDonald's chairman Ray Kroc.

1972 — The Egg McMuffin hits the McDonald's menu, making the breakfast sandwich a nationwide favorite.

WE DARE YOU!

An egg sandwich is great on its own, but a sandwich savant like you is probably ready to take it to the next level. Think you can handle the weird, the gross, the amazing, and everything in between? Here are just a few out-there options to experiment with . . . if you dare!

MAPLE SYRUP

SRIRACHA

MARSHMALLOWS

JALAPEÑO MUSTARD

PICKLE RELISH

RADISH

SPAGHETTI

BRUSSELS SPROUTS

CHOCOLATE CHIPS

BANANAS

EGG SALAD

Egg salad is easy to make, and there's good news for sandwich-lovers everywhere — an egg salad sandwich is just as easy! Take basic egg salad, slap it between two slices of bread, and you're good to go. You can also dress it up however you'd like — adding lettuce and tomato to your sandwich, or spicing up the egg salad itself. Try adding curry powder to your egg salad recipe for a unique take on the traditional recipe.

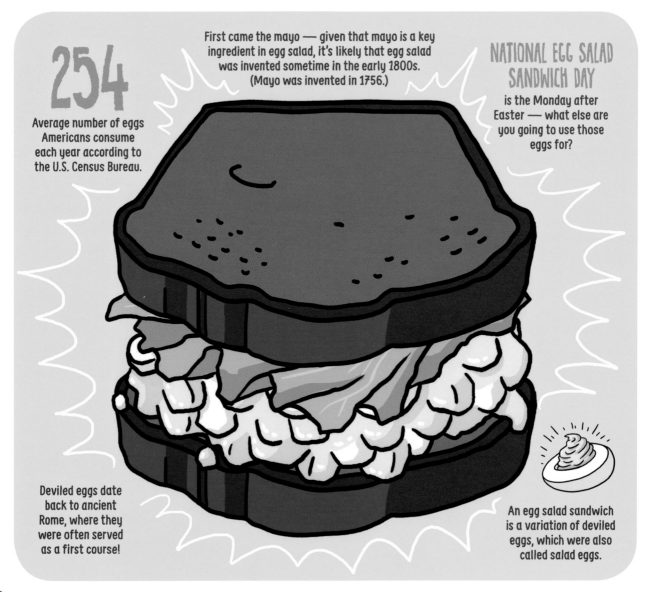

254

Average number of eggs Americans consume each year according to the U.S. Census Bureau.

First came the mayo — given that mayo is a key ingredient in egg salad, it's likely that egg salad was invented sometime in the early 1800s. (Mayo was invented in 1756.)

NATIONAL EGG SALAD SANDWICH DAY

is the Monday after Easter — what else are you going to use those eggs for?

Deviled eggs date back to ancient Rome, where they were often served as a first course!

An egg salad sandwich is a variation of deviled eggs, which were also called salad eggs.

WHEAT BREAD

Swap out the bread entirely and opt for a pita pocket — easier to eat on the go.

Or try it in a lettuce wrap!

LETTUCE

Spice it up with
HOT SAUCE!

You can also spice up your sandwich by adding:

PICKLES

EGG SALAD

CHEESE

BELL PEPPERS

WHEAT BREAD

Make your sandwich open-faced by skipping the top piece of bread!

Egg salad is easy to customize. Try adding thinly sliced green onions or finely chopped celery for extra crunch and color. And if you don't like mayo, Greek yogurt is an easy substitute!

BASIC EGG SALAD

In a medium saucepan, cover 6 eggs with at least an inch of water. Bring to a boil and remove from heat. Let the eggs sit in the hot water for 15 minutes, then run them under cool water.

Peel and chop the eggs.

Mix with:
1/4 cup mayo
1 tablespoon mustard
Salt and pepper to taste

Refrigerate for at least an hour.

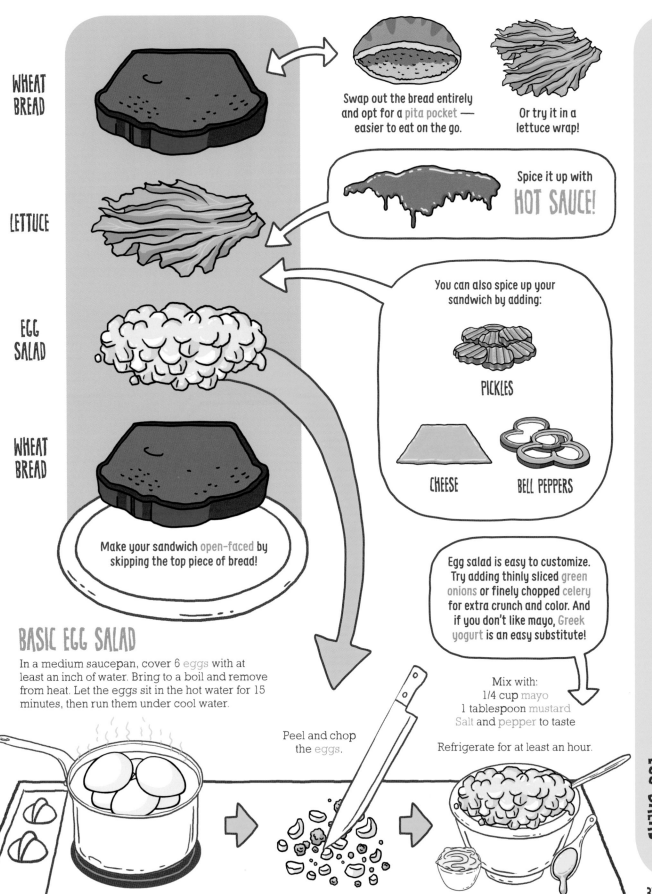

FLUFFERNUTTER

The unofficial sandwich of Massachusetts, the fluffernutter is perfect for sandwich-lovers with a serious sweet tooth. Made from sweet marshmallow fluff (hence the "fluff") and creamy peanut butter (hence the "nutter") this sandwich is delicious when eaten for dessert, or even lunch if you're looking to switch it up from your standard PB&J.

1917

MA

Marshmallow Creme is invented by Archibald Query in Somerville, Massachusetts. He originally sold it door-to-door.

OCTOBER 8

NATIONAL FLUFFERNUTTER DAY falls on October 8th. Somerville, Massacusetts, still celebrates an annual Fluff Festival.

1913

Amory and Emma Curtis of Melrose, Massachusetts, invent Snowflake Marshmallow Creme.

The term "fluffernutter" can also be used to describe other sweet treats made with marshmallow fluff and peanut butter.

1960

The Durkee-Mower advertising agency coins the term "fluffernutter" so they have an easier way to market the sandwich.

WHITE BREAD

White bread is traditional for this soft, sweet sandwich, but you can also use wheat.

You can also get strawberry flavored fluff in some regions of the U.S.!

MARSHMALLOW FLUFF

What is marshmallow fluff? Melted marshmallows and corn syrup blended together to create a spreadable treat.

I DARE YOU!
Add potato chips to your fluffernutter if you're feeling adventurous or try sliced bananas for a tamer option.

PEANUT BUTTER

ALMOND BUTTER

Peanut allergy? No problem! Just substitute another nut butter (like almond butter) in its place. You can also try this sandwich with Nutella.

NUTELLA

WHITE BREAD

Wash it down with a cold glass of milk.

FLUFFERNUTTER

39

ICE CREAM

I scream, you scream, we all scream for ice cream! — ice cream sandwiches, that is. No meal would be complete without dessert, and no sandwich cookbook would be complete without an ice cream sandwich. You can customize this frozen delight any way you like. You pick the cookies, you pick the ice cream, you pick how many you can eat before brain freeze sets in.

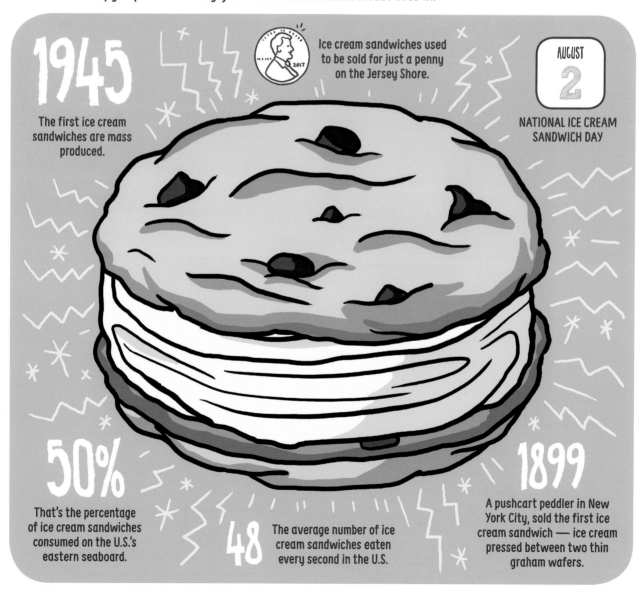

1945
The first ice cream sandwiches are mass produced.

Ice cream sandwiches used to be sold for just a penny on the Jersey Shore.

AUGUST 2
NATIONAL ICE CREAM SANDWICH DAY

50%
That's the percentage of ice cream sandwiches consumed on the U.S.'s eastern seaboard.

48
The average number of ice cream sandwiches eaten every second in the U.S.

1899
A pushcart peddler in New York City, sold the first ice cream sandwich — ice cream pressed between two thin graham wafers.

CHOCOLATE
CHIP
COOKIE

ICE CREAM

CHOCOLATE
CHIP
COOKIE

DID YOU KNOW?

This ice cream sandwich is technically called a Chipwich — ice cream sandwiched between two chocolate chip cookies — and was invented in 1981 by Richard LaMotta in New York City.

Make sure your ice cream is soft enough to scoop and spread, but not so soft it melts.

YOU PICK THE FLAVOR —
any type of ice cream will do!

VANILLA

CHOCOLATE

STRAWBERRY

MINT CHIP

Refreeze your sandwich as a whole once it's assembled.

Once you have your ice cream sandwich assembled, try rolling the edges in chocolate chips or sprinkles — they'll stick to the ice cream.

ICE CREAM

41

S'MORE

Ready for s'more sandwiches? You don't need summer, or a bonfire, or marshmallow-roasting sticks to enjoy this sweet treat. You can whip up this campfire-inspired sandwich in the comfort of your own kitchen, no open flame required. Just be prepared to make extra, because we can almost guarantee everyone will want s'more.

1927

The first published recipe for "Some More" appears in *Tramping and Trailing with the Girl Scouts.*

90 Americans buy 90 million pounds of marshmallows a year — the equivalent of approximately 1,300 gray whales.

AUGUST
10

NATIONAL S'MORES DAY

A "Graham Cracker Sandwich" recipe appeared as early as 1920. At that time it was already popular with Boy Scouts and Girl Scouts.

423 The Guinness World Record for the most people making s'mores at one time. The record was set in Huntington Beach, California, on April 21, 2016.

1938

The contraction "s'more" first appears — it's in a publication aimed at summer camps.

WHITE BREAD

PRO TIP!

Butter both sides of the bread before grilling. Feeling fancy? Try dipping the butter side of the bread in graham cracker crumbs before grilling it for a more authentic tasting s'more.

GRAHAM CRACKER CRUMBS

You can use real marshmallows, but we recommend using marshmallow fluff or creme — it will melt and warm up much faster.

MARSHMALLOW FLUFF

CHOCOLATE

Use Nutella in place of chocolate for a different flavor.

WHITE BREAD

Try adding peanut butter to take your s'mores sandwich up an extra notch.

Grill your sandwich for a couple minutes on each side, until the bread is golden-brown and the toppings are gooey.

Try it with a veggie dog — a great camping companion for your sweet campfire treat!

NUTELLA AND BANANA

Are there any two items that pair together better than Nutella and bananas? (Well, maybe peanut butter and jelly, but that's a different story and a different sandwich.) This rich, creamy hazelnut-cocoa spread is best served warm, so we recommend grilling up this sandwich on the stove. Serve with an ice-cold glass of milk to wash it all down!

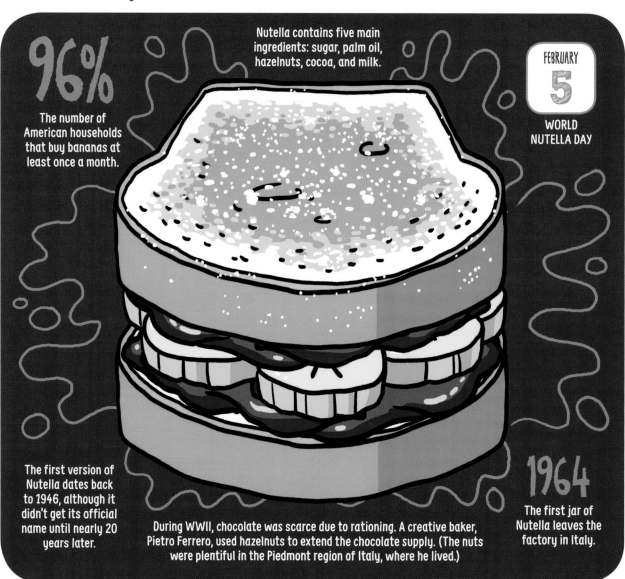

96%

The number of American households that buy bananas at least once a month.

Nutella contains five main ingredients: sugar, palm oil, hazelnuts, cocoa, and milk.

FEBRUARY
5
WORLD NUTELLA DAY

The first version of Nutella dates back to 1946, although it didn't get its official name until nearly 20 years later.

During WWII, chocolate was scarce due to rationing. A creative baker, Pietro Ferrero, used hazelnuts to extend the chocolate supply. (The nuts were plentiful in the Piedmont region of Italy, where he lived.)

1964

The first jar of Nutella leaves the factory in Italy.

FRENCH BREAD/CROISSANT

Don't forget to butter the outside of your bread before grilling! (This will only work on flat bread, not a croissant.)

NUTELLA

SLICED BANANAS

NUTELLA

FRENCH BREAD/CROISSANT

BANANA SPLIT!

Try adding the following ingredients to your ooey, gooey sandwich to make it even more delicious:

PEANUT BUTTER

STRAWBERRIES

PINEAPPLE JELLY

HONEY

CINNAMON

SHREDDED COCONUT

Grill your sandwich for a couple minutes on each side, until the bread is golden-brown and the toppings are gooey.

Dust your sandwich with powdered sugar before eating.

APPLE PIE

There's nothing like a warm slice of homemade apple pie. Now imagine you could hold that pie in your hand and enjoy it for lunch. Thanks to this apple pie sandwich, you can! To make things easy, you can use store-bought apple pie filling, or if you're feeling fancy try making your own. (Just remember to ask an adult to help you when you're using knives or the stove.)

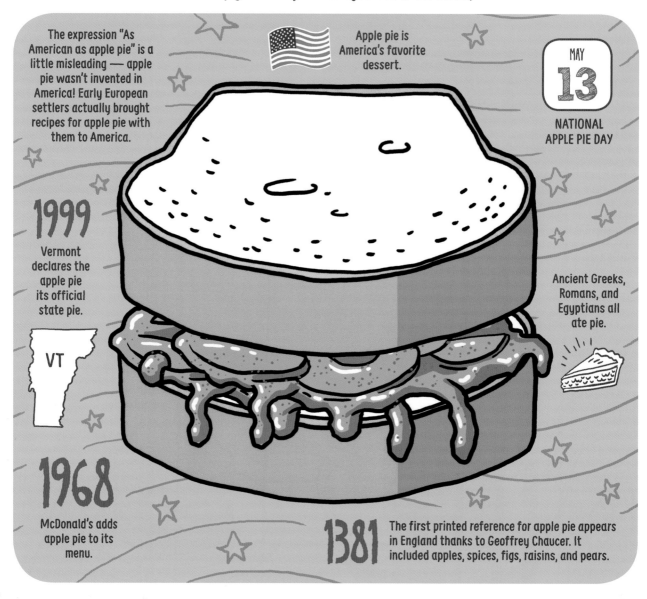

The expression "As American as apple pie" is a little misleading — apple pie wasn't invented in America! Early European settlers actually brought recipes for apple pie with them to America.

Apple pie is America's favorite dessert.

MAY
13

NATIONAL APPLE PIE DAY

1999

Vermont declares the apple pie its official state pie.

VT

Ancient Greeks, Romans, and Egyptians all ate pie.

1968

McDonald's adds apple pie to its menu.

1381 The first printed reference for apple pie appears in England thanks to Geoffrey Chaucer. It included apples, spices, figs, raisins, and pears.

WHITE BREAD

PRO TIP!
Make sure to choose a sturdy bread for this sandwich — once the apple pie filling heats up it'll be warm and gooey.

Skip the cinnamon sugar and add Cheddar cheese to your sandwich for a savory twist!

CINNAMON SUGAR

APPLE PIE FILLING

Add peanut butter to your apple pie sandwich to make it creamier.

WHITE BREAD

You could also just buy apple pie filling in a can, but let's be serious.

APPLE

Serve this sandwich à la mode — with ice cream!

Mix all ingredients together and heat on the stove for 15–20 minutes, until the apples are soft. Make sure to let it cool slightly before adding to your sandwich.

APPLE PIE FILLING

1 Tbs. maple syrup

1 Tbs. lemon juice

3 medium apples, peeled and sliced

2 Tbs. brown sugar

1 Tbs. flour

1 tsp. cinnamon

This filling is so good you'll want to eat it with a spoon! (That's okay, no one will be the wiser.)

ALISON DEERING, AUTHOR

Originally from Michigan — the Mitten State! — Alison learned the value of a good book and a great sandwich early on. After earning a journalism degree from the University of Missouri-Columbia, she started her career as a writer and editor. Alison currently lives in Chicago, Illinois, with her husband, where she makes, eats, and talks about as many sandwiches as humanly possible.

If Alison were a sandwich, she would be a fancy grilled cheese, inspired by the Grilled 3 Cheese at Café Muse in Royal Oak, Michigan.

WHOLE GRAIN BREAD

HAVARTI CHEESE

TOMATO

BASIL

HONEY

FONTINA CHEESE

MOZZARELLA CHEESE

WHOLE GRAIN BREAD

BOB LENTZ, ILLUSTRATOR

Bob is an art director who has designed and illustrated many successful books for children, and is the latter half of the duo Lemke & Lentz, creators of *Book-O-Beards*, part of the Wearable Books series. In his spare time, he likes to talk about food, especially sandwiches. Bob lives in Minnesota, with his wife and children, where they go for long walks, sing old-timey songs, and eat ice cream with too many toppings.

If Bob were a sandwich, he would be "The Snowpig," proudly hailing from Morty's at Hyland Hills Ski Area in Bloomington, Minnesota.

FRENCH BREAD

SRIRACHA

SWEET AND SPICY PICKLES

APPLESAUCE

PROVOLONE CHEESE

PULLED PORK

FRENCH BREAD

READ MORE

Gleeson, Erin. *The Forest Feast for Kids: Colorful Vegetarian Recipes That Are Simple to Make.* New York: Harry N. Abrams, 2016.

Hoena, Blake and Katrina Jorgensen. *Ballpark Cookbook The American League: Recipes Inspired by Baseball Stadium Foods.* Ballpark Cookbooks. North Mankato, Minn.: Capstone Press, 2016.

Jorgensen, Katrina. *Beat the Wheat!: Easy and Delicious Wheat-Free Recipes for Kids With Allergies.* Allergy Aware Cookbooks. North Mankato, Minn.: Capstone Press, 2017.